GIVEN

Anna E. White

ROYAL PRIESTHOOD
PUBLICATIONS

4GIVEN
ISBN 979-8-218-45389-3

Published in association with Royal Priesthood Publications.

Editor: Jasmin Anthony
thickthreadediting@gmail.com

Contents

Contents Continued

Preface

This is my personal testimony of my encounter with my Lord and Savior, Jesus the Messiah. He has delivered me and set me free from same sex attraction. I am forgiven.

I am sharing my story so that I may encourage someone else to know and experience the hope, freedom, love, and forgiveness that only Jesus can give.

"The Spirit of the Sovereign Lord is on me, because He has anointed me to proclaim good news to the poor. He has sent me to bind up the brokenhearted, to proclaim freedom for the captives and release from darkness for the prisoners (Isaiah 61:1; NIV)."

CHAPTER ONE

THE BEGINNING

The Beginning

Every story has a beginning. The beginning can be messy, disturbing, deep, and even dark. Sometimes it can leave a stain or a mark. This is the story of how my beginning shaped me and as a result led me down paths that I did not particularly want to take.

I grew up in a Christian home. As an infant, my mom took me to church. She even tried to convince the church we went to, to baptize me. They said no. They told my mom that they could not baptize me until I was old enough to understand; that it had to be a decision that I made.

I do not have many memories of when I was a little girl. I do remember the name of the church I attended was Tried Stone Baptist Church of Detroit, MI. This church was beautiful with stained glass windows and an intricately painted ceiling.

I remember going to Sunday School. My Sunday School class had beautiful artwork, portraying pictures of Bible Stories on the walls. I remember that I loved going there and that the people were nice to me.

I remember having dinner in the Fellowship Hall, a place with good food and even better conversations. We would eat there after the church service ended. I loved eating the church's sweet potato pie. It was so delicious.

One time during church, I was sitting behind this lady. While the pastor was preaching, she started shouting and jerking her body from left to right. She shouted so hard that her wig flew off her head and landed in the aisle. My four-year-old eyes stayed glued to this lady, watching her movements, not grasping what it all meant. I only took my eyes off her to see where her wig had landed.

When my eyes roamed back to the lady, I saw what had been underneath her wig the whole time. She had these tiny little braids sticking up out of her head like a field of twigs.

I looked over and saw this girl, who was about 9 or 10 years old. She and her friend that sat beside her were laughing at the lady. The girl started to mock the lady, overexaggerating the shouting and the movements. The next thing I knew this girl started shouting for real, crying truly sincere tears.

Three ushers of the church flocked around her with paper fans decorated with a picture of the church on the front of them. When the girl finished shouting and the ushers had left her side, her friend asked her what happened.

The girl only said these words: "It was real."

I just watched and took it all in. I learned that you do not play with God or the things of God.

One of my fondest memories is of a lady, whose name and face I cannot remember. I only remember what she asked me to do and the results of what she asked. One Sunday, she saw me standing in the fellowship hall with my mom.

She told my mom and me that she had stage four throat cancer and that she had to go into the Dr's so that they could perform x-rays. The doctors told her that she would have to have surgery. She then bent over, looked me intently in the eyes, and asked me to pray for her.

I smiled and said, "Ok."

That night, after I had dressed for bed. I kneeled beside my bed to say my prayers. I remembered the lady and prayed for her. The next Sunday, I wanted to tell her that I prayed for her, but I did not see her. I do not remember how long it was until I saw her again as I was about 4 or 5 at that time. Children have no knowledge of time.

I do remember that the next time I saw her she came running to me and she said, "You prayed for me, didn't you?"

I said, "Yes."

She said, "I know you did! The Dr's were going to do surgery on me but when I went in, they found no evidence of cancer!"

As a little girl that was amazing to me and I believed that if I prayed, God would answer me.

Chapter 2

The Move

The Move

At the age of five, my mom remarried and started to work at Eastern Michigan University as the Assistant Professor of Nursing. We moved to Ypsilanti, MI. into a new house in a new town where my sister and I knew no one. However, I was bold as a child; I had no fear.

There was a little girl outside when we pulled up into the driveway of our new house. She was our new next-door neighbor.

I said, "Hey, girl, come here!"

At the sound of my voice, she came over. I learned her name and we became the best of friends.

Since I lived in a Christian home, my mom was sure to find us a church to attend right away.

We started attending a church in Ypsilanti, MI. My mom became a member of the church right away, while my stepfather, my older sister and I simply attended.

It was at that church that I confessed the Lord Jesus Christ at seven years of age. I was baptized at that church.

I remember my mom saying, "Really! Are you sure!"

She was so happy, and I was so sure.

After she asked me if I was sure, I responded with a bold "Yes."

I walked down the aisle right after my stepfather had.

The pastor asked each of us if we believed that Jesus was the Son of God. We both responded with yes.

"Do you believe that He died, and that God raised him from the dead?"

Again, we said yes.

The pastor then welcomed us into the family and told us we would be baptized on the following first Sunday, where we would sit in a special section of the church auditorium for people who were just baptized, and that we would receive our very first communion.

After my baptism, things were not the same.

I remember playing outside with my best friend and the other neighborhood kids.

Before my baptism, I did not mind the things that they would do. I thought it was funny and cool. After my baptism, I did not enjoy those activities that used to make me laugh.

Instead of joining in on the fun, I would feel conviction and the urge to tell a grown-up.

One day when I was about eight years old, my best friend and the other kids were hanging outside her house underneath the carport. I rode over on my big wheel and saw them all together talking quietly.

When I got up from my bike, I realized they were talking about me. The whole gang of neighborhood kids had turned on me because I would tell my mom about the wrong things they did and then my mom would speak to their parents.

All the kids, including my best friend, decided they were not going to be my friend anymore.

My best friend told me, "I am no longer your friend. You are a tattle tale. I will only be nice to you when my mom is around and that is it. We are no longer friends."

I was heartbroken and I left in tears. That was the day I stopped talking as much. Every time I saw the other kids my head would naturally fall. I began looking at the ground as I walked. I decided that I did not want to be different anymore and that I wanted to have friends.

The name of the elementary school I attended was West Willow Elementary school. It was a few blocks away from my house and within my neighborhood. I walked to school every day.

Soon I became friends with other kids on other blocks. The other kids would stop off on the way to school at a house called Mr. Foster's.

My mom taught me not to visit strange places, like the houses of people my mom did not know.

Still, one day I tagged along to Mr. Foster's with my school friends when I was not supposed to be there. But, because the other kids went and I wanted friends, I went.

There was a side door, where all the kids would enter. Entering through the side door led to stairs, which led to the basement. As I walked down the stairs to the basement of Mr. Foster's house, my eyes got big!

Mr. Foster's basement was a candy store! There was pop, and chips, and every candy imaginable! My favorite was watermelon and sour apple Now and Later. We would go there every day before and after school.

To keep up with this activity however, I would have to have money. I began stealing from my stepfather's wallet every day. This was not a challenging thing to do since he was so unorganized with his money. He balled up his money in his pockets; never counting a thing. I would just take a couple of dollars and go to Mr. Foster's every day. I would buy it for me and my friends if they wanted anything.

Another occurrence that happened to me at the age of eight was that a neighbor's dog would bark at me every time I passed his house. Once when the neighbor was outside with his Doberman Pinscher, I passed by his house and again, the dog barked at me.

The neighbor, who was Caucasian, looked at me and said, "Did you know that dogs can see colors?"

I shook my head "no."

I stood there, nervously listening to whatever else the man had to say.

He said, "Well, they can. They hate the color black. If you don't want him to get you, you better stay from in front of my house."

I quickly ran to school.

After school, I went to Mr. Foster's as usual. When I was leaving there to go to my house, I crossed the street before I came upon the neighbor with the Doberman Pinscher's house. I hurried past there to my house.

Around that same age, certain kids at school bullied me.

My older sister, who attended high school, was known for fighting. I hatched up a plan. I started telling the kids at my school that if they did not leave me alone, I would get my

big sister.

It worked.

Eventually, my mom found out that

some kids at school were bullying me. She

made my sister walk me to and from school

until it stopped.

Chapter 3

I Just Want to Fit In

I Just Want to Fit In

There was nothing else I wanted back then, but to fit in. I wanted it so badly as a child that I began to act like the other kids around me, do what they did, say what they said. If they cursed, I cursed so that I could be cool and fit in with them.

I remember the first time I cursed. The kids around me looked at me and said, OOOOOOOO!"

I thought for sure, now I would be cool, but no. They still rejected me.

Then I started getting into trouble at school by my teachers.

Back in those days, the teachers could paddle you for misbehaving in class. Once during class I was talking to a kid who I wanted to be my friend. The teacher hit me with her paddle and told me to be quiet.

Yet, I kept on talking.

It did not bother me at all to get in trouble at school if the other kids liked me. If that was not bad enough, I continued this line of thinking in other areas of my life.

Since I was already stealing money to go to Mr. Foster's house to buy candy and pop for me and my friends, it became easy to sneak things out of the house.

I snuck out my frogger game and took it to school. By the end of the day my teacher confiscated it. The teacher told me that I had to

have my parents write a note to get it back. Fear

and panic set in.

Oh no, I thought. Now what am I going

to do?

Slowly a plan came into play.

My mom had pretty penmanship and it

was specific to her and hard to duplicate. My

stepfather, on the other hand, had the most

awful penmanship. I used to practice writing

like my stepfather because his penmanship was

so horrible.

Since I knew just how to write like him,

I wrote a letter to my teacher and forged his

signature. I got my Frogger back, but I also

found myself falling deeper into sinful behavior and destructive thought patterns.

There was a boy in my class that I really liked. His mom and my mom used to think we were so cute together. Not only were we in the same classes at school, but we went to the same church and attended the same Sunday School class. We used to talk all the time.

One day, he pulled me aside.

He said, "My mom and your mom think that when we get older, we'll be together. Let's get them. Let's not ever get together."

I said, "Ok."

Inwardly, my heart sank.

I was just a little girl, and the concept of boyfriends and girlfriends had not crossed my mind. All I knew was that I loved hanging out with him and thought he loved hanging out with me.

However, when he said that we would never get together, something in me broke. I felt like there must be something wrong with me if he wanted to show our parents that we would never get together.

I did not really understand why at the time, but I was really hurt by that. That hurt lasted a long time. I did not tell anyone. I kept it to myself.

Chapter 4

Evangelism

Evangelism

Around this age, my mom would call me in the kitchen to practice what she called soul winning.

My mom was over the Evangelism ministry at our church. She would go door to door evangelizing telling people about Jesus. She would knock on their door. When they opened the door, she would begin her script, which she had practiced with me.

My mom would say, "Do you know if you died today that you would go to heaven?"

She would prompt me to "say no."

I would say, "No."

She would then say, "If I showed you how you could know, would you do what the Bible says do?"

She would say, "Say yes."

I would respond, "Yes."

She would then go through the Romans Road with me. The Romans Road is a pathway of scriptures to show people where they are and lead them to Christ.

First, she would say, "In Romans 3:10: it is written, 'There is none righteous, no, not one:' Romans 3:23: 'For all have sinned and come short of the glory of God' Romans 5:12: 'Wherefore, as by one man sin entered into the world, and death by sin; and so death passed upon all men, for that all have sinned:' Sin has an ending ... it results in death. Romans 6:23a:

'For the wages of sin is death;' We all have

sinned and owe this wage of spiritual death. Did

you know that God loves you? Romans 5:8:

'But God commended his love toward us, in

that, while we were yet sinners, Christ died for

us.'

"When Jesus died on the cross, He paid

sin's penalty. Salvation is a free gift from God to

you! Romans 6:23b: '... but the gift of God is

eternal life through Jesus Christ our Lord.' You

can't earn this gift. You must ask and receive it.

You must ask God to forgive you and save you.

Romans 10:9-10: 'That if thou shalt confess

with thy mouth the Lord Jesus, and shalt believe

in thine heart that God hath raised him from the

dead, thou shalt be saved. For with the heart

man believeth unto righteousness; and with the

mouth confession is made unto salvation.' Like

any gift it must be received! Romans 10:13:

'For whosoever shall call upon the name of the

Lord shall be saved.'

"Are you ready to admit to God that you

are a sinner?"

I would say, "Yes."

She would say, "You need to believe in

Jesus Christ and that He is God's Son. Do you

believe?"

I would say, "Yes."

She would say, "You need to confess

your faith in Jesus Christ as Savior & Lord."

Then she would ask if I wanted to receive Jesus Christ as my Lord and Savior. I would say yes and then we would pray.

"Lord, I know that I am a sinner and need your forgiveness. I believe that Jesus died for my sins. I want to turn from my sins, and I ask you Jesus to come into my heart and life as my personal Savior. I will trust and follow you. You are my Lord and Savior. Amen."

Chapter 5

My Dad

My Dad

If someone asked me how my relationship with my mom was, I would say great. We had a wonderful relationship. In all honesty my mom was my greatest friend.

If someone asked me about my relationship with my dad, I would not have said much other than shrugging my shoulders.

My dad lived in Ann Arbor, MI. My mom used to call him up so he would spend time with me. He would oblige, come by, and take me out because of that.

I remember a time he took me out to lunch and I ordered a Shirley Temple to drink. It tasted so good. The base of the drink was 7UP with red stuff called grenadine at the bottom of the glass. A little umbrella sat on the edge of the glass. A maraschino cherry was in the glass. I loved that. I loved going to the park with him or going out for ice cream.

As I grew older, I perceived what was really going on. I would notice all the times my dad came to visit me were after my mom had called him. The only thing causing him to come was not his love and adoration for me, but obligation, so I began to not want my dad to visit me.

When my mom would ask me to call him, I would call him, but I really did not want to talk to him. I believed that if he knew where I was, if he wanted to talk to me, he would call.

The problem was I was making all the calls, putting in all the effort.

I thought, "Why doesn't he call me? I am a kid. Why should I be calling him? He does not care about me."

I had a stepfather, as I stated previously, after my mom remarried when I was five years old. However, at the time of their marriage I struggled trying to find what to call him.

My mom decided that I would not call him by his first name because that would be disrespectful. She then thought about me calling him dad. She thought long and hard about it, and then called me to the living room one day. My stepfather was there too. My mom did all the speaking.

She said, "I do not want you to call him dad because you already have one of those. I want you to call him father."

I could not fathom that. I wonder if I looked taken aback or shocked at that moment. For some reason, it made me feel extremely uncomfortable. Therefore, I never called him anything.

I would refer to him as my stepfather when talking about him to someone else. When I was just talking to him, I would go to where he was and begin talking.

I never had a real connection with him. I wanted one. I wanted him to be my dad, to love me like a dad should. But through that meeting I knew that would never happen. My mom and her new husband had drawn a line of separation when they told me what I should call him.

When it came to discipline, my mom disciplined me. My stepfather was not allowed to discipline me whatsoever. If I was grounded, my mom would ground me. If I was whooped, it was by my mom.

He was simply a man that lived in my house, my mom's husband, who went to church with us and was a treasurer at the church.

Although I had no connection with my stepfather, there were many ways I got to know him.

One of these ways was by stealing money from my stepfather's pockets to go to Mr. Foster's. Soon enough I would find other items in his pockets, like condoms. It was so

gross, and finding them was not restricted to just

his pockets.

He lost his keys all the time. One time

my mom asked me to look around to help him

find them. I looked in his coat pocket and what

was there? Keys? No, condoms.

I would look in the car under the seat

and in the glove box, and what was there?

Condoms. Everywhere I looked, I found

condoms.

I formed the opinion that he was a dirty

old man. This opinion shaped all my

experiences with him from that point forward.

I remember going to ask my stepfather a question for my mom and I had grape flavored ChapStick on my lips.

As I was talking to him, he said, "Have you been drinking grape Kool-Aid?"

I said, "No."

He said, "Your breath smells really good."

I backed up a little and my nose cringed. He did not see my reaction because he was looking at his computer. His comment scared me and from then on made me not want to be around him.

Chapter 6

Another Opinion Formed

Another Opinion Formed

When I was nine years old, my mom was pregnant with my younger sister. My stepfather worked for the State of Michigan as an auditor and his hours were nine to five. He worked in Detroit, MI which was a forty-five-minute drive away from the house.

However, on this day, the day my mom's water broke, he did not come home until one o' clock in the morning. At the time, I was staying at the next-door neighbor's house; my ex best friend, who hated me still, and her family.

I remember the moment when my mom's water broke. My mom, older sister and I were in our house. We were sitting around the kitchen table. When my mom stood up to get something, all this water came splashing down on the tile floor and formed a pool between her feet. It ran off underneath the chair I was sitting in.

My mom attempted to call my stepfather. When she could not reach him, she played with the idea of my sister driving her to the hospital, but my sister did not have her driver's license yet.

Instead, my mom sent my sister next door to have our other neighbor, Mr. K, take her to the hospital. My mom did not want me to come along, so my mom sent me to stay at the neighbor's house.

I stayed up all night looking out of my ex best friend's window.

From her window, I could see the driveway to my house. I watched my stepfather pull into the driveway, read the note posted on the door and leave. I knew then that he was cheating on my mom. I became angry and formed yet another opinion concerning men.

Children perceive more than their parents believe they do.

Chapter 7

Last Year of Elementary School

Last Year of Elementary School

When I was in fifth grade, I had a boyfriend. He had a brother. They both were extremely cute. I was happy to have a boyfriend. We must have gone together for about a week.

One day after school I saw him. He called me over. As I walked toward him, he grabbed me and threw me up against the wall. Then he pulled me forward so that I was on top of him, and his brother came behind me.

Those brothers did to me what dogs have done to the legs of humans. I did not know what to think or what to feel. I was dazed, I guess. I never really processed what took place and never talked about it to anyone. I just acted like it never happened, but it was memory that hurt my heart.

If there was anybody I could have told, I would have hoped it could be my sister, but my older sister and I had a different kind of relationship. We are seven years apart. So, when I was a kid, I had one job and that was to leave her alone and not talk to her. If only she knew how much I admired her.

This girl started a dance team and competed in competitions. I was in awe of her and wanted to be like her.

I once walked into her room uninvited and unannounced, and she was reading a book while doing a handstand!

Another time, I walked into her room uninvited and unannounced, she was sitting on the floor with her leg wrapped around her neck!

She was so cool and amazing! She had friends that were cool too!

One day, my mom went to Bible study in the evening, as was her norm. My older sister and I were home. I was downstairs trying to sneak a sip of Faygo Rock and Rye Pop.

That was my absolute favorite soda back then. My mom used to freeze them, so it had been thawing in the refrigerator downstairs. I snuck down the stairs to open the pop.

I was just going to take a little sip. Because the pop had been frozen, when I went to unscrew the top, it exploded like a volcano and pop went everywhere! I did not know what to do so I ran up the stairs to my sister's room.

Lo and behold there was a boy in there! I immediately ran back out of her room and called my mom on the phone. I told her everything that happened, except for the details that incriminated me.

In the meantime, the boy dressed and came out. He patted me on my head and left out the front door.

All I could do was cringe. He had touched me without even washing his hands! Yucky!

My mom came home, fussed at my sister, and spanked her. My sister ran out of her room. When my stepfather came home, he fussed at my sister too. In addition to the fussing, he punched her with his fist. It was awful.

My mom yelled at him to stop.

My sister curled herself into a fetal position and pulled out chunks of her own hair. It was horrible!

After the events that happened that day, my sister started running away from home.

Every time my sister ran away, my mom went out, found her, and brought her back home. That would only last temporarily. When my sister got a chance, she would run away again. She hated my stepfather. Who could blame her?

She finally got away when she chose to

join the Navy. I, on the other hand, was very sad

to see her go. She used to teach me how to

dance. When she left, I stopped dancing.

Chapter 8

Middle School

Middle School

In middle school, I no longer needed money for Mr. Foster's. I now needed money for school activities, so I kept on stealing my stepfather's money.

At this point I felt justified. In my eyes, he deserved it because of all the horrible things he did.

One day, as I was in my mom's bedroom, I started poking around in my stepfather's dresser drawer. I found all his Playboy magazines. I was shocked as I had never seen anything like that.

What did I do?

First and foremost, I did not tell my mom about this brand-new discovery. Second, I decided this discovery would make me cool to the other kids at school.

I took them to school and showed them to the kids on the school bus.

My ex best friend was on the school bus. She still would not speak to me. When she saw what I was doing, she rolled her eyes, turned her nose up, and turned her head in the other direction. I did not care because I had the attention of everyone else.

I snuck the dirty magazines onto the school bus every day for a whole week.

Then one day, the bus driver slammed on the brakes of the bus. She looked like she was about to come to the back of the bus where I was.

I quickly snatched up all the magazines and threw them out of the bus window. My ex best friend just looked at me with a hard face. The shenanigans on the bus only got wilder from there on.

In ninth grade, I was sitting in the middle of the bus, trash talking and making fun of a boy who was dark in complexion.

You know how kids make "yo mama" jokes. That boy was telling "yo mama" jokes at me. I did not do "yo mama" jokes.

I came back with another quick reply, "You so black that when it's dark outside you have to smile for anyone to see you."

The boy got so angry. He stood up, pulled down his pants, and showed me his private parts.

All the boys shouted, "Yeah!" "That's it! You showed her!"

The feelings and emotions that I had were inaccessible; I was not completely in tune with them. By then, I was an expert at suppressing things and keeping things to myself that I really do not know.

I do believe that the actions that boy took on the bus can leave a person with shock and fear.

Even though I could not access my emotions then, I must have been shocked; taken back by what the other boys were saying and what that boy had done.

Chapter 9

Liar, Liar

Liar, Liar

Over the years, I watched my stepfather deceive and cheat on my mom.

It was crazy. I never understood how a person could lie the way he did and expect people to believe the untruth that was so plainly false. It was amazing.

For a time, he would cheat every Monday. Cagney and Lacey would come on TV, and he would not come home.

The worst part was that the lie he told at that time never changed. He always had a flat tire and could not make it home. He would use this lie for months at a time.

Eventually, my mom would get upset and say something.

My stepfather would bring her flowers, apologize, and he would be home for about 2 weeks, acting on his best behavior.

And then, when he had gotten bored or tired, he would be off again cheating. Albeit he would change the day he stayed out all night on. Instead of Monday, he would run out and cheat on another day, say Saturday.

I remember one Sunday my stepfather came to church putting his clothes on!

He had stayed out all night Saturday cheating and came to the church the morning after.

He walked into the church, scrambling

to put on his suit jacket. His shirt was hanging

out of his pants. He tucked his shirt in as he

walked down the aisle. Amazing. All of his

shenanigans were comical and sad, but nothing

could prepare me for what happened next.

Chapter 10

Mom Diagnosed with Cancer

Mom Diagnosed with Cancer

When I was fifteen years old, the doctors diagnosed my mom with cancer.

My mom and I were close. At this age she began to confide things to me.

She asked me if I wanted to know why she and my dad were not together.

Out of curiosity, I said yes.

She told me that she would tell me if I promised not to hold what she said about him against him.

I said I would not hold it against him.

She began to tell me that they had gotten a divorce because my dad held a shot gun to her

head while she was pregnant with me. My dad
told her that he was going to kill her.

She also shared with me information
about my older sister's dad and why they had
divorced. She told me how she had come home
from work one night and found him in bed with
another woman.

Back then there used to be chains on the
inside of the doors.

She said that the chain was on the door,
but that she could see through to the bedroom.
My mom saw him dressing and handing the
woman her clothes as he shoved her out of the
window.

At that time, my mom stayed in an
apartment. That apartment had stairs that led to

the ground level, so this woman left out the window to go down the stairwell and safely to the ground.

All these experiences that my mom shared with me formed thoughts in my mind concerning men.

I said nothing to my mom, but I was angry. Maybe my promise of not holding anything against my dad or the men that hurt my mom was thinner than I had thought?

One day, I went to use the restroom in my house, but forgot to lock the door. My stepfather walked in on me.

Instead of closing the door and apologizing, he decided he would have a full-blown conversation with me while the door was open.

I became more afraid of him, despite my stepfather never touching me inappropriately. However, because of my experiences and age, how I viewed him shaped my thoughts and actions toward him.

I remember when my mom's cancer began to worsen. I came home from school and found her on the floor.

I asked her how long she had been there.

My mom told me she had been on the floor since nine o' clock that morning. She had fallen while trying to take herself to the bathroom. She had been on the floor ever since. I got home at 2:30 that afternoon.

This angered me. Here my mom was, needing help, but my stepfather refused to let anyone help her. I let the emotions build up and spill over.

I went to the bathroom, looked in the mirror, and just kicked back. I put my foot straight through the wall.

Later, when my stepfather asked me how the hole got there, I lied.

I said it got there because I had fallen backward and my elbow went through the wall.

My stepfather said, "It looks like a foot to me."

I said, "Nope, it's an elbow."

He stared at me as if he knew I was lying. However, I kept my poker face on. After all, I had learned it from him.

Eventually, my mom ended up in a wheelchair.

I remember watching my stepfather bump her into walls. He did not allow my mom's sisters to help. He did not want to hire any nurses.

All during this time, he continued with his infidelity and was active member at our church. This formed a strong opinion in my mind that church people were nothing but hypocrites.

My mom was the only one different. She was a strong woman. She made sure I did everything I was supposed to do like choir practices, organ lessons, school rehearsals and the like even though she was not feeling well.

She dealt with her cancer diagnosis while attending classes in the Doctorate Program at Wayne State University. She was the first Black woman admitted into the doctorate program. She completed that program.

My mom is amazing. (I say this because she lives on in heaven.)

When I was sixteen years old, I lost my mom to breast cancer. I was in the eleventh grade.

I was still in church at the time.

When you are a child, you go where your parents go. I went to the church in

Ypsilanti until my stepfather stopped taking me, which was about three months after my mom had passed.

I remember being so angry with God.

I knew at an early age that God hears me, and He listens to prayers. I had prayed and asked Him to heal my mom or take her out of her misery.

Well, when she passed away, I was mad at God for taking her away from me. When I had prayed that God would take her out of her misery, I had not wanted Him to take her away from me.

I did not want to talk to God anymore.

I was full of so much bottled-up anger and rage. It was bottled-up so tight that I screamed and stomped my feet.

After I released a little of the aggression, I put the top back on my bottle of pain, looked up to heaven, and flipped God off. I knew better than to say anything out of the way or crazy to Him.

Funny how I still had enough respect for Him not to curse Him with my mouth. I did not have enough respect for Him to fall on my knees, tell Him about all that plagued me, give Him all my cares and concerns, or even receive His love. At this point, I really believed that I should never open my mouth to pray.

If I could have what I said when I prayed, then I could potentially ruin the very life I wanted to keep. I also believed there was no one in the entire world who could love me. The only one who did love me, God took away from me.

I wiped the tears from my face, sniffed up the snot and walked away. I continued in my life as if nothing had happened.

Chapter 11

Kicked Out

Kicked Out

One morning, I was moving too slowly for my stepfather. He wanted me to braid my younger sister's hair for school. I was still in the bathroom getting ready for school myself.

My stepfather decided he would set the microwave timer for three minutes. I was supposed to take my bath in that amount of time.

Three minutes is not a long time; I did not make it. He began to yell at me and tell me to get out.

I told him I was not finished in the bathtub yet. He told me he was going to come in anyway.

I said, "You can't because I'm naked."

He came to the door and tried to unlock the door. I jumped out of the tub and pressed my body firmly up against the door while my feet slid from all the water on the tile floor. I was screaming and yelling at him not to open the door. He started banging on the door with his fist and trying to come in on me.

You cannot imagine what went through my mind. I was scared and I could not understand why he was going to come in there, especially when I told him I was naked.

What was he going to do to me? What if he got in? I was naked and he was going to see me. He eventually gave up trying to bust the door down. However, his anger had won.

He kicked me out of the house.

My stepfather went into my room, got my house keys from my dresser, and told me to get out.

He took my little sister and left the house, slamming the front door behind him. I waited for a while before leaving the bathroom. What if he came back? What if this was a trick to get me to come out of the bathroom?

When I finally did come out of the bathroom, I called two of my aunts and told them what had happened and asked if I could come live with them. One said she could not afford to take me in. The other said she had to talk it over with her husband, but she could at least pick me up and take me someplace safe.

I waited for my aunt to get me. While I was waiting, there was a knock on the door and then the doorbell rang.

I said, "Who is it?"

The voice on the other side of the door said, "It's your father."

Confused, I opened the door. It was my dad. When he stretched out his arms to hug me, I fell into him.

I said, "How did you know to come?"

He said, "Your Aunt called me."

He had me get all my things and I left to go live with him.

I loved my dad, but I never wanted to live with my dad. I wanted to live with my aunt; the one who needed to check with her husband.

According to her, her husband had said no. She called up my dad. For some reason, he came. However, I had not seen or talked to my dad in years.

While I lived with my dad, he wanted me to attend a different school other than the one I was currently attending.

Of course I did not want to change schools. Who would want to start a new school when they graduate next year?

I had a boyfriend at this time as well, whom I had started talking to before my mom had passed. She knew his dad and we all went to the same church.

My mom would not allow us to go out on dates or anything because she believed I was too young. My boyfriend and I were only allowed to talk on the phone. He went to a different school anyway.

After much coaxing, my dad allowed me to finish my junior year at my school. However, things quickly changed after that.

That summer, I went to visit the aunt whose husband said I could not stay with them. I loved my cousins and wanted to spend the weekend with them.

I called my dad to ask if I could stay the weekend. He said yes. I ended up going to camp with my cousins.

At the end of camp my aunt showed up with a big black garbage bag. I looked in the bag and what did I see? All my belongings! My dad had put me out and for what?

I called him and asked him what was going on.

He said, "You don't want to be here anyway."

So, he dumped me out on the very aunt who already said she could not keep me. Great, rejected again.

My aunt still could not keep me. My dad did not want me. Somehow, I ended up moving back in with my stepfather. This is when I lost connection with my boyfriend.

Chapter 12

The Start of Same Sex Attraction

The Start of Same Sex Attraction

My stepfather continued in his illicit activities. Every Friday, he would take my younger sister and go to his lady friend's house and leave me home by myself until Monday. In the meantime, what was I supposed to do? I struck up a friendship with a girl I met.

It started off innocently enough, as she filled the void I had for my mom. I began to spend a lot of time with her, writing her notes, and talking on the phone. I felt a connection with her that I had been missing with everybody else.

Overtime, I began to have sexual urges toward her. It felt normal to me, although I had never felt that way before.

One day, while she was over, we were talking in the kitchen, and I was sitting at the counter. She was standing close to me in front of my legs. We were laughing and talking and then we drew near to one another and kissed.

We both jumped because neither of us had planned that. We were best friends and that was all.

In shock I said, "Are you ok?"

She said, "Yes."

She said, "Are you ok?"

I responded, "Yes."

I asked her, "Did you like that?"

She responded, "Yes."

She asked, "Did you like that?"

I responded, "Yes."

We kissed again.

She would come over on the weekends or evenings that my stepfather was not home.

We both attended the same high school. I was a senior and she was a junior. We even had certain classes together, like choir. We spent every moment we could together.

Since we were spending so much time together and kissing every chance, we awakened sexual desires in our bodies. One weekend when we were alone, we engaged in activities more heated than kissing.

In the moment I asked, "How could something that feels so right be so wrong?"

She said nothing.

My question showed that I knew that what I was doing was wrong. Everything I was doing was only based on the way I felt. It gave me pleasure to give into these feelings.

Everyone that sins, sins because they get pleasure from it. If it did not feel good, we would never do it.

Chapter 13

Disassociation and Hatred of Males

Disassociation and Hatred of Men

During the same time, there was a boy that kept chasing after me. He wanted to be my boyfriend. I did not like him. I was with someone else.

I thought however that he would make a good cover for me. That no one would figure out that me and the girl I was with were more than best friends.

I arranged to meet up with the boy. We talked in his car, discussed sex. I told him that I was not going to have sex before marriage, and he agreed, saying he had made the same decision.

One day, he came over to my house. I had invited him over because he kept harassing me about being his girlfriend and yet never being able to come to my home to visit with me. He came over and what was supposed to be a fun time turned sour.

He raped me on my kitchen table. I kept telling him no. He did what he wanted anyway, pulled down my clothes and forced himself upon me.

My mom's picture was on the wall right in front of where he was raping me. I wish I could have covered her soft, kind eyes so she would not have to watch this violent struggle. It was as if her glowing memory was cracked, tainted by the agonizing desires of this boy.

He got off me and then laughed.

It was not funny to me. He deeply hurt me. My screams had gone unheard. What made matters worse, he had raped me right in front of my mom (even though it was just a picture).

After he left, I went to the bathroom and took a shower.

The police will tell you not to take a shower after a rape. It would erase all the evidence and DNA. If you chose to report the rape, it would be the other person's word against yours.

I did not think about this. At this point I had developed a lifestyle of not telling and just going along with whatever.

The girl I was seeing at the time came over after the boy had raped me. I was clearly shaken up. We were teenagers so we did not know what to do. She tried to comfort me the only way she knew how. Of course, that was not what I needed or desired.

After what happened, I wondered if I even liked men. I purposely set out to see if I liked them.

One guy I tried this hypothesis on, I did not even know. He was the brother of a friend of mine. They lived down the street from me in the cul-de-sac. I was a senior in high school, and he was in college.

My friend called me up and said he was home and that her parents were gone. My stepfather had taken my little sister and left me home alone for the weekend. Off I went, down the street. When I entered the house, my friend told me where to go.

When I got to his room, all the lights were off. It was dark and the room reeked of alcohol. With this stranger, I performed my experiment. I never saw his face.

I did not like what I did with that guy. I thought he was gross and disgusting. Therefore, I formed an opinion, said "yuck," and decided that I must be a lesbian. This reaction was based primarily on my experience with this guy, the faceless stranger. I continued in the lifestyle that gave me comfort.

Every weekend while my stepfather and little sister were at his lady friend's house, I would either have my girlfriend over or I would stay at her house. Every chance we got we were together. We were in a relationship for four years.

During that same time, my stepfather and I found ourselves in this endless loop. He would kick me out of the house, someone from my family would talk to him, and I would end up back at the house. This happened until I graduated high school.

Meanwhile, there was a lot that happened in my relationship with that girl, whom I called my best friend and first love.

Toward the end of our relationship, her mom increasingly came between us. Her mom loved her and that was evident in her actions. Her mom sat her down and talked with her candidly about what we were doing and how it was wrong. She even told her that she could hear us upstairs every night, while we thought we were in a world of our own hidden and secluded from others.

She was incredibly open and honest with her daughter. She expressed to her how wrong our relationship was and explained to her daughter that what she was doing was not who she was. I hoped she would not listen to her mom because I had intense feelings for this girl.

What her mom was saying had never been brought up in our conversations before. Her mom never spoke to me about being a lesbian. She never tried to approach me to say that what I was doing was wrong and not who I was.

She did not do this because she did not know me. She saw me as the perpetrator not as someone that needed love.

This mom did not go to church. As far as I knew, she did not have a relationship with God or knew the love of Jesus for herself. Therefore, I could never expect her to help me.

What she did to me, instead, was for about a month every week, would put about six nails in my tires.

They lived on a dirt road so in the beginning, when I first started noticing the nails in my tires, I thought I must have been driving over the nails. It was the mom of my best friend and girlfriend.

She was angry with me for having a relationship with her daughter. She confessed her anger towards me and that she had put the nails in my tires right before she kicked me out of her house.

She arranged for me to stay at her friend's house. Her friend kicked me out of the house too after I came home plastered from a night of drinking.

I was on a downward spiral and had no clue what to do.

After high school, I moved from one friend's home to another friend's home. There was not any stability for four years.

I had another best friend. I was not physically attracted to her, but she was attracted to me. She always wanted me to come over. For a while, I enjoyed seeing her and hanging out, but then things changed.

The more I went over to her house, the more opportunity allowed for me to be alone with her brother. When I was alone with her brother, he raped me.

After the first time, this became consistent. Every time thereafter when I went to her house, her brother raped me. Every single time I went to visit her, her brother raped me.

I figured I should not tell my friend because it would cause a rift between us. I could not tell anyone in her family because who would believe me?

It did not matter what I had to say, what I felt or what I wanted. The idea formed that people were going to do what they wanted to do despite my feelings, needs, or wants. In this, I learned how to disassociate from people, specifically men when something unwanted happened to me. I learned how to disconnect in my mind.

If I felt threatened in any way or if someone tried to take my body, I said to myself "he may take my body, but he will not take my mind."

From the age of 17 to 26, I lived my life

as a lesbian. I believed that was who I was. I

had feelings and desires for women. Most of all,

I hated men. I thought all men were disgusting.

The negative relationships that I had had with

men supported my beliefs.

Chapter 14

Living the Life – I Want Out!

Living the Life- I Want Out!

Over the years, I was in and out of relationships. None of them seemed to last too long. I could say that no matter what I did to try to make them work, they just did not work.

In all these relationships, I did crazy things. My lifestyle was unhealthy. I was unhealthy. I was more miserable than I was happy. I experimented with drugs and drank excessive amounts of alcohol. I manipulated people, lied to people, lied about people, got into fights.

One fight I recall being involved in was not my fight, but a fight between a friend of mine and another girl. One night out on the town my friend saw her girlfriend out at the gay

bar we were at. My friend became angry when

she saw her girlfriend with someone else.

With all kinds of vulgarities spilling out

of my friend's mouth, she headed for her car.

The other girls with us and I followed her to her

SUV. When we got to her car, she got her gun

out from under the seat. She said she was going

to kill her girlfriend.

She tried to cock the gun. I was in front

of her. She was pointing the gun at me. She

tugged hard on the gun trying to cock it. She

pulled with all her might.

I stood there in front of her, thinking

"Please, don't let this gun go off on me."

When I look back at my lifestyle as a lesbian, I know I was never happy. It is not what God intended when He created males and females. Therefore, all my relationships with women were doomed from the start.

At the age of twenty-six, I remember praying to God. I was tired of living life as a lesbian. I was not sure if change or freedom was possible, but I really wanted out. I began to pray Psalm 51:

> *"Have mercy upon me, O God,*
>
> *According to Your lovingkindness;*
>
> *According to the multitude of Your*
>
> *tender mercies, Blot out my*
>
> *transgressions. Wash me thoroughly*
>
> *from my iniquity, And cleanse me from*

*my sin. For I acknowledge my
transgressions, And my sin is always
before me. Against You, You only, have I
sinned, And done this evil in Your
sight— That You may be found just when
You speak, And blameless when You
judge. Behold, You desire truth in the
inward parts, And in the hidden part You
will make me to know wisdom. Purge me
with hyssop, and I shall be clean; Wash
me, and I shall be whiter than snow.
Make me hear joy and gladness, That the
bones You have broken may rejoice.
Hide Your face from my sins, And blot
out all my iniquities. Create in me a
clean heart, O God, And renew a*

*steadfast spirit within me. Do not cast
me away from Your presence, And do not
take Your Holy Spirit from me. Restore to
me the joy of Your salvation, And uphold
me by Your generous Spirit. Then I will
teach transgressors Your ways, And
sinners shall be converted to You. O
Lord, open my lips, And my mouth shall
show forth Your praise. For You do not
desire sacrifice, or else I would give it;
You do not delight in burnt offering. The
sacrifices of God are a broken spirit, A
broken and a contrite heart— These, O
God, You will not despise.* (Psalms 51:1-
4, 6-13, 15-17 NKJV)

After this, I had an experience with God. He showed up while I was engaging in my sin, and I knew I had done wrong. I hid my face from Him, like Adam and Eve in the garden of Eden when they had sinned.

Later, I said, "God if that was really you, you will show up again."

Well, do you know what happened? He showed up again in the middle of my sin. Again, I knew I had done wrong, so I hid my face from Him. Again, I felt like Adam and Eve in the garden of Eden when they had sinned. Again, I said, "God if that was really you, you will show up again."

Except this time, He did not show up.

I said, "That was God!"

I said I was not going to have same sex relationships anymore. I went to the church I had belonged to, rejoined, and recommitted my life to Christ. I did not participate in same sex activities or live life as a lesbian for five years.

Chapter 15
One Foot In, One Foot Out

One Foot In, One Foot Out

Although I had rejoined the church and recommitted my life to Christ, I lived a life neither hot nor cold. I did not attend prayer service or Bible study. I did not attend church services on a regular basis. I went to Sunday school and church when I felt like it.

Then, out of nowhere, at the age of thirty-one, I had a really strong sexual desire, and I didn't know what to do. I tried to overcome the feelings, but I struggled. I became strongly attracted to one of my female friends.

I called my cousin who lived life as a lesbian. I asked her to hook me up with someone. I knew that if I was in a relationship with someone else, I would not want to pursue my friend.

My cousin would not set me up with anyone. She knew I had recommitted myself to Christ, so she refused to hook me up with anybody.

However, after six months of hounding my cousin, asking her repeatedly to hook me up with somebody, I finally convinced her. She delivered. I met the woman my cousin had set me up with. Instantly, we developed a sexual relationship.

After a week, I got a call from my godmother, whom I had asked to be my mom a year prior.

She asked me, "What are you doing?"

I told her exactly what I had been doing. She said, "You know you're wrong."

As soon as she said those words, my eyes opened. There was a struggle with what I knew was right and what my body wanted. My mind knew it was wrong, but my body craved those things I should not have.

I could not sleep. I could not enjoy physical intimacy. I would try to break up with my girlfriend. We would break up, moments later I would call her right back, apologize with tears and weeping, and then we would get back together.

This struggle lasted for months. I was on a rollercoaster ride. I was nauseous and could not get off. I tried to talk to the pastor at my church that the time, but he was unavailable.

As time went on, I was so embarrassed that I did not want to talk to anyone anymore. I just delved back into the lesbian culture.

I went to gay pride parades. What was interesting was I did not enjoy them. I found them lewd and vulgar. Even though I was participating, I found certain things to be wrong and disagreeable to me such as parading in the street half-naked. I kept those things to myself and continued doing what I was doing.

One day, my cousin asked if I wanted to go to a gay parade in Chicago. While in Chicago she said she was going to get a tattoo and her tongue pierced. Other girls I knew were going as well.

My cousin dared me to get a tattoo and my tongue pierced with her, calling me Square if I did not join her. I did not want to be a square, so I said I would go. Since my cousin had dared me, I also said I would get a tattoo and my tongue pierced.

At this time, I lived in Kalamazoo, MI. We only had to travel two and half hours to get to Chicago. In Chicago, we watched the parade, but I was disgusted inwardly.

My cousin said, "Look there is a tattoo and piercing place! Let's check it out!"

We all followed her to the tattoo and piercing shop.

I had been thinking about what I would get in my mind long before we had gotten to Chicago. I did not need to look at pictures on their walls or flip through books on their counters because I had already planned on getting a tiger paw print with rainbow colors on the paw prints.

Suddenly, a thought came to my mind. It said, "What if you change your mind?"

I believed these were my own thoughts, and so I thought to myself, "I can't change my mind. I came here with my girls, and I said I would do this. I must do this!"

Another thought came to mind, "What if that is not who you are?"

Perplexed, I began to think about how tattoos are permanent. Permanent could never be erased, much like what I thought of the pains of the past which I still held tightly to.

So, I walked over to the area of the shop where they had pictures of different tattoos in these binder books. I began to flip through them. As I flipped through the pictures, I came across a cluster of Chinese symbols with pretty leaves underneath and wrapped around the symbols. Written on the right-hand side of the picture were the words, "Faithful, truthful, and loyal."

The thought came to mind, "That is who you are."

So, I chose that picture. I could not afford the entire tattoo as it was $300, and I did not have the money at the time. I did, however, get the symbols. I put it on my lower back.

I got my tongue pierced too. I went first because the others were chickens.

I did not know it at the time but that entire conversation that I had in my mind where I went back and forth over what tattoo to get was significant. It had been the Lord speaking to me. And I, in turn, had been speaking to Him.

Chapter 16

Tell Me the Truth!

I began to visit gay churches, searching for the truth or someone to say what I was feeling and doing was normal. Yet I could find no one to tell me that. No one could validate my actions or feelings.

I had only one question: Is it ok to be gay? No preacher in the gay community would answer that.

Sure, people living that lifestyle would tell me it is ok. They had no other choice. If it were ok for me, it would be ok for them too.

The preachers that I spoke to would say, "I can't tell you that, you have to be the judge."

I thought that was so interesting. I was looking for acceptance and validation, but they were saying "we can't tell you if it's right only you can judge."

That caused me to think and see that the way I was living was not right. I really wanted and needed to seek and know the truth.

At this point, I was pretty turned off from church. I stopped going when no one would tell me the truth. I became irritated, cynical, and sarcastic. I concluded that I hated churches, and anything related to church.

I was still in a relationship with the woman that my cousin had introduced me to. She liked to play the drums and had heard that this one church was having service in the park.

She wanted to go but I did not. She said she wanted to play the drums at the church's event. I told her to call them and see if they'd let her. She called the church and spoke to the minister of music, who told her to come to the Church in the Park event and that they would see what she got.

I laughed at her. I knew that was just a ploy to get her to join the church. They weren't going to let some girl they did not know or met come and play the drums at their church.

She asked me to go with her. I decided I would go just so I could say I told you so when they did not allow her to play. We went. When we arrived at the park, there was a huge tent set up and tons of folding chairs. The church had brought out their actual pulpit and all the

musical equipment for them to have church

there. I was shocked.

The minister that my friend had spoken

to was there. He told her to have a seat in one of

the folding chairs.

She said, "I want to play!"

He said, "You will."

I found a seat and sat down near the

organ, near where the choir was. We stayed for

the entire service.

It wasn't until church was over that the

minister let her play the drums. I had never

heard her play before.

The minister of music said that she was

good. He invited her to come to an actual church

service. She wanted to play for the church, so we went the following Sunday.

It was now August of 2003. I still did not want to go to church. I did not want anybody to know about my same sex relationship. Plus, knowing I was wrong to be engaged in that lifestyle, I did not want to be a hypocrite like the other people in the church.

I knew I was not going to change. I did not want to pretend to be someone I was not. I ended up going only because my friend really wanted me to go.

Somehow, I ended up joining the church. I started attending Sunday school, prayer service, and bible study. I went to their new members' classes, and I even joined the choir.

126

What in the world was happening to me? I really enjoyed going and hearing the Word of God. Whenever the pastor would preach or teach, I would find myself regurgitating what he said to friends and family members. I was getting God's word in me, though my personal life was far from Him.

At home, I had started to distance myself from my friend. We lived in a two-bedroom apartment. I moved out of the room we shared and stayed in the other room.

Suddenly, I began to see things. When she looked at me, red eyes stared back at me. I got scared. When I went to my room, I would put things against the door so she could not come in.

One night, I woke to this thing that resembled a black and white cat sitting at the foot of my bed. Its face was like a cat; it had a long tail with a point on the end and the bottom of its feet appeared to be hooved.

Its sudden appearance in my room startled me. I jumped. I rubbed my eyes and looked again, it jumped down, ran off. and I never saw it again.

Chapter 17

God Speaks to Me

God Speaks to Me

One Sunday, when I went to church, one of the preachers preached his farewell sermon. I have no idea what that preacher preached. At the end of his sermon, everyone was standing and saying, "Amen!"

I stood up along with everyone else except that while they had been listening to the preacher, I was hearing the voice of God.

He told me, "I have a great work for you to do. You cannot do it with her here."

I began to cry and rejoice at the same time. My response was "Yes Lord."

That was all I could say again and again, "Yes Lord, Yes, Lord, Yes Lord."

No one thought anything of it because it was happening while the preacher had been preaching. The people, shouting and rejoicing about whatever the preacher had been saying, drowned any noise I made.

I was not quite sure at that time what God was talking about concerning the great work He had for me. However, I knew that the woman I was in a relationship with had to go. Simply because God said so.

As soon as we got back to the apartment that day, I told her that she had to go. That was no easy task.

She resisted.

She wouldn't pack her things. She said she wasn't going. She called the minister of music at the church to see if he could find somewhere for her to stay. She even asked him to stop me from putting her out. I could not give in to any ploy she tried because I knew that God had given me specific orders. I had to carry them out. Eventually, my friend found no other choice but to leave.

I took her to her hometown in Detroit, MI. It was a two- and half-hour drive from Kalamazoo.

The minister of music and other people at the church were calling the phone I had bought her nonstop, so I took it from her, turned it to silent, and hid it away until I dropped her and all her things off at her aunt's house in Detroit.

When I had gotten on the freeway back to my apartment in Kalamazoo, I answered the phone. It was the minister of music.

He tried to talk me out of taking her back to Detroit. But his motives seemed to be shady. I felt like he was trying to get in my business. So, I did what anybody who didn't want their business out would do; I told a half-truth, which is a lie.

I told him that she liked me, not that the feelings were mutual. I also told him that God wanted her to go back to her hometown. The minister of music backed off from the issue.

I thought that everything would be fine after that, once I had done what God had said. I thought it was over. I thought I would never

have to deal with this again. Boy was I wrong!

Chapter 18

Not Over Yet

Not Over Yet

I struck up another friendship with another woman at the church. We hung out all the time. She became my best friend.

I was so excited to finally have a real best friend. So, imagine my surprise when I became attracted to her.

"Oh no! What is going on," I remember anxiously thinking. "This is not what I want, especially not from her this is my friend! I need some help!"

I confided in her about my same sex attraction. I could not confess that I was now attracted to her.

"What would she think of me," I thought. "What would become of our friendship? Surely, she would abandon me!"

One day it all came to a head on the night I slept over her house. We started wrestling. We were having fun until thoughts began to invade my mind, telling me to grab her and kiss her.

I wrestled silently in my mind telling the thoughts, "No, this is my friend."

The thoughts became louder and more frequent, almost like it was trying to force me to grab and kiss her. I was so confused.

Part of me wanted to act on what I was feeling. Yet I could not compromise.

We continued wrestling. By this time, she was sitting on top of me. She had my hands pinned over my head, laughing.

I remember shaking my head and whispering, "Jeeeeeesuuuuuus!"

In my head, I was screaming. I was in so much turmoil. While my friend was wrestling with me, I was having the fight of my life in my own mind. My friend had no idea I was thinking these thoughts about her.

Knowing that her roommate was next door, and she was sitting right there on top of me, I found the predicament I was in painful. I didn't want anyone to know that I was a lesbian because I did not want to risk losing our friendship, be ridiculed, talked about, shunned, or once again rejected.

I did not desire those invading feelings, but I also did not know what to do or how to stop them. All I could do was whisper Jesus' name.

Suddenly there was calm in my mind. The thoughts I had been having, the thoughts of touching her, grabbing her, kissing her, ceased.

The next day, I called my friend and asked her and her roommate to pray for me. From going to church, prayer service, and bible study, I learned that where two or three are gathered Jesus would be in the midst.

I did not think I could pray for myself. My rationale was that I was this awful person so surely God would not listen to me.

My friend invited me to her apartment so that she and her roommate could pray with me. When I arrived at my friend's house, I never received that prayer. Instead, I received condemnation. I received a nose turned up at me, scriptures told to me. I was belittled and yelled at.

Her roommate told me she had seen me wrestling with my friend in the room. It had happened while the door was open. My friend and I were playing; it was innocent. We were not doing anything inherently inappropriate so there had been no reason to close the door.

The roommate was angry with me. She irately told me how the Lord gave her Romans chapter one verses sixteen through thirty-two to read and how she wondered why she was meditating on that scripture.

She said, "Now I see why God had me meditating on these scriptures. It was you!"

Her roommate handed me a King James Bible and said, "Here! Read it!"

I sat down in a chair and read the scriptures, while my friend's roommate stood over me. I could not understand what I was reading.

At that time, I had been back in the church for a short while. Plus, she had given me a King James Bible. I was a baby Christian who could not understand King James' version of the Bible on a good day.

My friend's roommate yelled at me, "Of course you can't understand it. You are blind and living in darkness! You asked us to pray for you, you don't want to change. If you did, you would tell your pastor!"

I felt horrible! I was ashamed. I was hurt. All I wanted to do was leave. I was supposed to receive prayer, but they never prayed for me.

Did these ladies know my heart? They both went to church. Did they not have the spirit of God living in them like they said? Would God tell them that I did not want to be this way,

that I wanted to change? What just happened
here?

I left with a lump in my throat, fighting
back tears because I refused to let that woman
see me cry. I got in my car. When I had gotten
only a few blocks away, I had to pull over. I just
broke down and cried. It was ugly.

I cried out to the Lord and asked Him,
"WHY WAS I TREATED SO HORRIBLY
WHEN I WANT TO CHANGE AND AM
SEEKING HELP TO DO SO? WHY WAS I
REJECTED AND MADE TO FEEL LIKE I
AM OR HAVE A DEMON YET THERE WAS
NO PRAYER FOR ME? WHY GOD WAS I
TREATED THIS WAY WHEN YOU KNOW
ALL I WANT TO DO IS SERVE YOU AND

LIVE RIGHT BEFORE YOU? WHY DID THIS LADY WHO IS SUPPOSED TO BE A MINISTER IN TRAINING AND HAVE YOUR SPIRIT INSIDE OF HER RESPOND TO ME THIS WAY?"

After I finished crying out to God, I cleaned up my face and sat there with the car still running. A thought came to my head about what the roommate had said.

She had told me that if I was serious, that I would have talked to my pastor.

Initially, I had responded in my mind, "So he could reject me? No, I wouldn't."

This time as I was reminded of the roommate's words, I responded with, "I will call him first thing in the morning."

Chapter 19

Breaking Free

Breaking Free

I was serious; I wanted to change. I hated being the way I was.

That Tuesday morning, I called the church office and was able to get in to see my pastor that day. I told him everything that had happened. I remember saying, "Aren't you going to lay hands on me and cast this demon out?"

He simply said this, "Say you have a cut or a wound on your hand, you must put medicine on it. It's the medicine that helps it to heal."

I just looked at him, lost and confused, so he broke it down for me further.

He called me by my first name and said, "Sin is a wound. You must apply the word of God to your wound if you want to be healed."

Still, I looked at him blankly, only blinking both eyes.

The pastor said, "Read the word."

I said, "I know what it says, it says it's wrong."

He said, "Have you read it where it applies to your situation?"

I said, "No because I know it says it's wrong."

He said, "Read it."

Then he prayed for me. I left his office and went on my way.

I went home and decided I was going to get rid of everything and everyone from my past. I erased every phone number to people associated with same sex attraction. I threw away all my clothes that looked boyish or reminded me of that lifestyle. Whatever had a rainbow on it, I threw it out.

I told my friend from church not to call me. I told her we could not hang out anymore because I needed God to help me. I said, "I'll call you when I'm available."

I told God that I was not going to eat anything or go anywhere or watch anything on TV unless it was about Him. I was not going to let Him go until He changed me.

Wednesday night I went to bible study.

After it was over, I went up to my pastor and

said, "Nothing has happened. It's not working"!

He looked at me and smiled and said,

"Keep the faith." So, I continued to read the

Bible. I looked up scriptures that had to do with

my situation.

Chapter 20

Forgiven

Forgiven

On Thursday, I remembered something someone said to me. It happened one time when my friend, her roommate, and I had gone out to eat. I remembered my friend's roommate say, "If you have an aught or a problem with someone, whoever they are and however many there are, write their names down on a piece of paper then next to their name write I forgive."

So, I wrote down their names. I filled up an entire sheet of paper with names. Who knew I had so many aughts?

I wrote the words, "I forgive" next to each name. I tore up the paper and prayed and asked God to forgive me. Then I went to bed.

On Friday morning, I got up and read scriptures again. I was getting discouraged. Previously, I had looked up and written down every scripture that dealt with lust and sexual immorality. I was reading what I already knew, which was that lust and sexual immorality were wrong.

As I sat there, I lifted my eyes and looked at the ceiling. I had a thought come to mind that said, "Read John." So, I turned to the Gospel of John chapter one and began reading. After I had been reading for a while, I had to go to the restroom.

So, I got up and began to walk down the hallway. It was there that God showed up. He appeared in the hallway of my apartment.

There was a big bright light! So bright that that was all I could see. I lost control of my legs and my body automatically fell to the floor. I used my arms to catch myself on the wall and landed in a kneeling position.

I looked into the bright light. I heard a voice, the voice of my Lord and Savior say to me, "I forgive you."

I burst into tears, wept uncontrollably. He said, "Read some more."

I got up from the floor, wiped the tears from my face, and used the restroom. When I got back from the restroom, I sat back on the couch and continued to read. I remember reading *and you shall know the truth and the truth shall make you free* (Jn. 8:32)."

Next thing I knew, these black cloud-like things floated upward off my eyes. The Spirit of God from within me began to rebuke the enemy out of my house. I don't remember what He said, but I remember His authority.

I remember his righteous indignation. I remember His passion for me. I remember He was not playing with the enemy. I remember that when He finished dealing with the enemy, I was free!

I knew the truth! I understood that same sex attraction was not from God and deliverance was mine.

After that, I felt hungry. I went into the kitchen to find something to eat. I opened the door of the refrigerator and as I was looking into the fridge a thought came, "As I gave John,

Mary, as his mother, so I have given you,

Calista (my friend from church), as your sister."

Oh, my goodness, I thought. I was so

excited, I jumped up and down and I ran to the

phone, called her, and told her everything. I also

told my pastor everything. I was so elated. I had

such joy that I could not explain. I was on cloud

nine and nobody could get me down or so I

thought.

Chapter 21

Staying Put

Staying Put

I thought everything was over, that I
could move on. But then, the thing I had
dreaded all along happened. Various individuals
began to find out that I had been a lesbian. They
started talking about me as if I was still in sin.

The story that was passed around was
that I had tried to start a relationship with my
friend, not the woman I had been in a
relationship with, the one I had driven back to
Detroit.

At this point, I was ready to run away
and find another church where no one knew me.
But God said, "No, stay where you are."

People at the church continued to talk
badly about me. They did not want my friend

from church to spend time with me. They did

not want us to sit together nor ride to church

together.

Some people began to talk about my

friend. They would say she must be gay to want

to be my friend, quoting "birds of a feather flock

together."

My friend did not know what to do. She

tried to run away, distance herself from me, and

not be friends. However, she decided to stay

because God told her to.

When she first told me that God told her

to stay, it angered me. I was going through so

much and she was supposed to be my friend.

She was not supposed to abandon me, or even

consider that as an option, if she were my best

friend. The only reason she stayed was because God told her to.

She should not have had to be made to stay by God; it should have been an automatic reaction to all the hate that came our way. But you know what? I praise God in that still. He intervened and caused her to stay and stand with me. It would have been a much more difficult road without her support.

Speaking of support, my Sunday school teacher was one of my biggest supporters. He was also instrumental in helping me to form new opinions about men.

One Sunday, I was sitting in the back of my Sunday School class kind of hidden. My Sunday School teacher was talking and noticed me sitting back there. In the middle of his sentence, he acknowledged me boldly.

He called me by my name and told me it was really good to see me. There was a white light emitting from his eyes. I recognized that the Lord was working through him. It made me blush, not at him, but the Lord.

After Sunday school, we always went to the fellowship hall for breakfast. I had finished eating and was on my way to the sanctuary for the service when I ran into my Sunday school teacher.

He made sure he got my attention. Once we had come closer to each other, he said he wanted to apologize and make sure I knew that he was not hitting on me. He assured me that he loved his wife, only spoke to me as a friendly gesture.

I told him that I knew that. He said he just wanted to make sure. I smiled so big and bright, but I think I did it more so on the inside. I remember thinking thank you Lord for allowing me to meet a man of integrity like him.

He was like a big brother to me. Because of his walk with the Lord, he helped me to understand and know that all men aren't gross, or care only for themselves, or hypocrites, or only wanted one thing. It was just some men, specifically, those who did not have a personal relationship with the Lord and who were not living for Him.

During this time, God sent someone else to me. I was shrinking back and talking less. I was starting to shy away. I was at that church because the Lord told me to stay, I was being watched. It was as if I was in some sort of prison.

So. God sent someone from a different church to deliver me a message. This woman approached me one day and said, "God sent me to give you a message."

I said, "OK."

She said, "He wants to know why you are sitting in prison when He has opened the doors and freed you?"

At this point, I had put up walls because of how other members of the church treated me.

I looked at her and just stared blankly into her eyes.

She said, "Do you not know what I am talking about?"

I just stared at her and shrugged my shoulders. I gave a slight head shake to say no.

She said, "That is really weird. Usually, when God sends me to someone, they know exactly what I am talking about."

Then it happened. The flood gates opened! Tears came rushing down my face.

I said, "They won't let me be free!"

She responded with, "Listen, God Almighty has set you free. Who are they?"

In an instant, my entire demeanor changed. I remembered what God had done and who I was. I began to run for the Lord. I have

been running for Him ever since.

Chapter 22

My Cloud of Witnesses

My Cloud of Witnesses

It was not until later I found out that there were select individuals that would stop the flow of rumors when it came to them. There had been certain people who stood up for me. I call them my cloud of witnesses.

Behind the scenes God was working in my favor and on my behalf. There seemed to be a lot of people talking against me. The truth is that there were only a very few.

I did not know there were more people working for me behind the scenes than people who were working against me. That was twenty years ago. I have been free for twenty years now. The Lord delivered me and set me free in

2004! Thank you, Lord, God!

Chapter 23

Renewing My Mind

Renewing My Mind

The difference between now and when I was 26 is that when I was 26 years old, I believed homosexual behavior was wrong and I stopped participating in it. I made a choice to not participate in a homosexual lifestyle any longer, but that did not work. It didn't work because I did not renew my mind.

The Bible says, *"I appeal to you therefore, brethren, and beg of you in view of [all] the mercies of God, to make a decisive dedication of your bodies [presenting all your members and faculties] as a living sacrifice, holy (devoted, consecrated) and well pleasing to God, which is your reasonable (rational, intelligent) service and spiritual worship. Do*

not be conformed to this world (this age),

[fashioned after and adapted to its external,

superficial customs], but be transformed

(changed) by the [entire] renewal of your mind

[by its new ideals and its new attitude], so that

you may prove [for yourselves] what is the good

and acceptable and perfect will of God, even the

thing which is good and acceptable and perfect

[in His sight for you] (Rom. 12:1-2) AMP.

Matthew 12:43-45 according to the NIV

says, *"When an evil spirit comes out of a man, it*

goes through arid places seeking rest and does

not find it. Then it says, 'I will return to the

house I left.' When it arrives, it finds the house

unoccupied, swept clean and put in order. Then

it goes and takes with it seven other spirits more wicked than itself, and they go in and live there. And the final condition of that man is worse than the first. That is how it will be with this wicked generation."

As a result of me cleaning my house and not filling it with the Word of God, the enemy came back with seven of his friends and I was worse off than before.

Chapter 24

To God Be the Glory

At the age of 32, being delivered from same sex attraction was something that I did not do. I can take no credit. Jesus did it.

You see, **I was dead in my transgressions and sins, in which I used to live when I followed the ways of this world and of the ruler of the kingdom of the air** (Eph. 2:1-2).

I lived among them at one time, gratifying the cravings of my sinful nature and following its desires and thoughts (Eph. 2:3).

I practiced homosexuality (lesbianism, same sex attraction) (1 Cor. 6:9).

But, I was washed; I was justified in
the name of the Lord Jesus and by the Spirit
of God (1 Cor. 6:11).

My transgressions have been forgiven
and my sins are covered (Rom. 4:7). I am the
righteousness of God (1 Cor. 5:21).

Therefore, there is no condemnation
because I am in Christ Jesus and He has set
me free (Rom. 8:1-2). I am not controlled by
my flesh, but by the Spirit, because the Spirit
of God lives in me (Rom. 8:9).

I have no obligation whatsoever to do
what the flesh desires (Rom. 8:12). My body
is a temple of the Holy Spirit, whom is in me,
whom I received from God. I am not my
own; I was bought at a price, through the

blood sacrifice of Jesus Christ. Therefore, I honor God with my body (1 Cor. 6:19-20) **and flee from sexual immorality** (1 Cor. 6:18).

Because of who Jesus is and what He has done, I am not ashamed of the gospel of Jesus Christ for it is the power of God unto salvation for everyone who believes (Rom. 1:16).

Notes to the Reader

Now that you have read my personal testimony, it is my hope that you saw the thread that runs through this book. Although in this book, I reveal how the Lord delivered me from same sex attraction, it is about so much more than that. It speaks to other areas of one's life too.

The thread that runs through this book is mindset. Everything that I went through was about how I thought or what others thought concerning me. Over time I learned that I am not responsible for another person's thoughts or actions towards me. However, I am responsible for my own thoughts.

What we think is what we will do. Our thoughts determine our actions. It is important what we think. Every day we encounter situations, circumstances, events, environments, and people. Those things help to shape our thoughts. Our thoughts can lead us on destructive paths if we do not renew our minds daily in the word of God. The Bible says in Romans 12:1-2 TLV:

[1] I urge you therefore, brothers and sisters, by the mercies of God, to present your bodies as a living sacrifice—holy, acceptable to God—which is your spiritual service. [2] Do not be conformed to this world but be transformed by the renewing of your mind, so that you may

discern what is the will of God—what is good

and acceptable and perfect.

It is my hope and prayer that from reading this book you desire to experience God for yourself; to seek to know Him and His will for your life with great expectation. Believe and trust that He loves you. He is with you. He will protect you. He will answer your prayers.

If you do not know Jesus as your personal Lord and savior and you would like to know Him, pray this prayer out loud:

God, thank You for loving me. You gave Your one and only Son Jesus for me. I believe in Him. I confess with my mouth, and I believe in my heart that Jesus is Lord. I surrender my life and all that I am and have to

Him. I confess and believe that Jesus died for

my sins and for the sin of the world and that

You, God, raised Him from the dead. Thank

You for creating in me a new heart and a right

spirit that is willing and obedient to you. In

Jesus' name. Amen.

 You are now a new creation in Christ!

Remember this day.

Sign____________________________________

Date____________________________________

Check this link out to find a local church body in your area:

https://www.rhema.org/index.php?option=com_wrapper&view=wrapper&Itemid=114

Please do not forsake the assembling of yourself together as is the manner of some. (Hebrews 10:25) You have received Jesus as Lord, make sure you check with Him on where to go. He will tell you. Trust and listen to Him.

Now that you have read my personal testimony it is my hope that you sense the love that God has for you. God loves you so much! You are not what you do, you are who God says you are. God desires a relationship with you. He desires to be close to you, closer than a brother. His love for you is great and unfathomable. I have never felt a love like His.

I have felt dirty, lonely, confused, angry, hurt, torn, bitter, enraged, sad, rejected, and dejected. I have been laughed at, scorned, ridiculed, talked about, turned away from, pointed at, and more. BUT GOD. When He forgave me, everything changed. People will be people. However, the love that I felt from Him is hard to explain. I can only say there is nothing in the world like it. Nothing.

Was I born gay? Is it ok to be gay? These are some of the questions I had. You know what? When I encountered Jesus, I found out the truth about same sex attraction and received the answers to those questions. Was I born gay or having same sex attractions? No, I wasn't. I was born like all others. The bible says, "For as through the one man's disobedience the many were made sinners." (Rom. 5:19)

Adam and Eve sinned against God and caused all mankind after them to be born into sin. Now all mankind sins. To sin is to miss the will of God. It is doing things our own way instead of His way.

At one time I denied God. I knew in my heart that what I was doing was wrong. But I justified it in my mind. I thought, "How could something that feels so right be so wrong." I pushed past those thoughts of doing the wrong thing and continued in what I was doing. The result of that was a seared conscious.

I still heard God in my thoughts and through people, but I no longer recognized that it was God speaking. I thought people were being mean to me and I began to twist scriptures saying things like God is a God of love and we are to love everybody. I took scriptures about God's love and twisted them to mean that I could love the same sex and that there was

nothing wrong with that. However, to sin is to

miss the will of God. I was in sin.

In the first book of the Bible, the book of

Genesis, we find the will of God regarding

males and females. Genesis 1:26-28 TLV:

> *[26] Then God said, "Let Us make man*
>
> *in Our image, after Our likeness! Let*
>
> *them rule over the fish of the sea, over*
>
> *the flying creatures of the sky, over the*
>
> *livestock, over the whole earth, and over*
>
> *every crawling creature that crawls on*
>
> *the land." [27] God created humankind*
>
> *in His image, in the image of God He*
>
> *created him, male and female He created*
>
> *them. [28] God blessed them and God*

said to them, "Be fruitful and multiply,

fill the land, and conquer it. Rule over

the fish of the sea, the flying creatures of

the sky, and over every animal that

crawls on the land."

God our creator, created us either male
or female. He did that. One of the purposes of
males and females is to procreate. It is the will
of God our creator for us to have children. Two
people of the same sex will never be able to
have children together. God designed the male
and female so that when they come together
sexually a child would come from the two being
joined together. That is the will of God.

So, is it ok to be gay? No, that is sin and sin is to miss the will of God. To have attraction toward the same sex is a sin because that is not God's will. It is God's will that a man desires a woman and for a woman to desire a man. Let's look at Genesis again. Genesis 2:18-22:

> *[18] 'And the Lord God said, "It is not good that man should be alone; I will make him a helper comparable to him." [19] Out of the ground the Lord God formed every beast of the field and every bird of the air, and brought them to Adam to see what he would call them. And whatever Adam called each living creature, that was its name. [20] So Adam gave names to all cattle, to the*

birds of the air, and to every beast of the

field. But for Adam there was not found

a helper comparable to him. [21] And

the Lord God caused a deep sleep to fall

on Adam, and he slept; and He took one

of his ribs, and closed up the flesh in its

place. [22] Then the rib which the Lord

God had taken from man He made into a

woman, and He brought her to the man.

[23] And Adam said: "This is now bone

of my bones and flesh of my flesh;

She shall be called Woman,

Because she was taken out of Man."

[24] Therefore a man shall leave his

father and mother and be joined to his

wife, and they shall become one flesh.

[25] And they were both naked, the man and his wife, and were not ashamed.

This passage covers several things. It covers LGBTQ, bestiality, pedophilia, polygamy, sex before marriage, etc. How can I say that you might ask. I say that because here we see God's will for human beings, for males, and females.

It is his will that a male and female desire one another, be joined together in marriage, have children whom they raise to know, love, and be in relationship with Him. This may not be what you want to hear, but it is what you need to hear. It is the truth. It can be difficult to leave this lifestyle especially if you

have been engaging sexually with someone.
Don't let that stop you from going after God or
desiring His will for your life. The first thing
you must have is the desire to change.

Jesus is waiting on you to come to Him.
Come, confess your sin to God. 1 John 1:9 TLV
says, "*If we confess our sins, He is faithful and
righteous to forgive our sins and purify us from
all unrighteousness.* God will forgive you and
help you through this if you want Him to. Your
part is to do whatever He tells you and to live
for Him and not you. Are you willing to do that?
If so, pray this out loud:

God, thank You for loving me. You gave
Your one and only Son Jesus for me. I believe
in Him. I confess with my mouth, and I believe

in my heart that Jesus is Lord. I now surrender

my life and all that I have to Him. I confess and

believe that Jesus died for my sins and for the

sin of the world and that You, God, raised Him

from the dead. I confess that I have been living

a lifestyle that is not your will. Thank you that

You forgive me and create in me a new heart

and a right spirit that is willing and obedient to

you. In Jesus' name. Amen.

You are now a new creation in Christ!

Remember this day.

Sign____

Date____

If you have prayed this prayer. It is now time for you to join a local church body of believers, if you do not have one, so that you may learn more about our Lord and Savior, and grow in knowledge, wisdom, and understanding of Him and the purpose He has for you. You have work to do, and it is not just existing in this life. There is so much more that God has for you. Here is a church locator link.

Check this out to find a local church body in your area:

https://www.rhema.org/index.php?option=com_wrapper&view=wrapper&Itemid=114

Please do not forsake the assembling of

yourself together as is the manner of some.

(Hebrews 10:25) You have received Jesus as

Lord, make sure you check with Him on where

to go. He will tell you. Trust and listen to Him.

Note to the One with a Friend or Family Member Struggling with Same Sex Attraction

Now that you have read my personal testimony of the forgiveness of God, I want you to know that God is not a respecter of persons. He has no favorites. What He did for me, He will do for others. Don't give up hope.

The Lord loves us all. He sent His Son to die for the sin of the world. As long as there is breath in our bodies, there is hope.

You may wonder, what can I do? The best thing you can do is to love unconditionally with healthy boundaries in place. You can also pray for them. When speaking to that family member or friend, the Bible says to speak the truth in love. Speak the truth with God's love, according to His Word, and who He says they are. Be led by the Spirit of God and be sensitive to His leading.

There may be times He will tell you to hold your tongue and pray only. There may be times when you are called to stand on the truth of His Word and face opposition for doing so. Your relationship with the Lord is of utmost importance. You are His sheep. Listen to His voice and follow Him.

If you do not have a relationship with Jesus or know Him as your personal Lord and savior and you would like to have a relationship and know Him, pray this prayer out loud:

God, thank You for loving me. You gave Your one and only Son Jesus for me. I believe in Him. I confess with my mouth, and I believe in my heart that Jesus is Lord. I surrender my life and all that I am and have to Him. I confess and believe that Jesus died for my sins and for the sin of the world and that You God raised Him from the dead. Thank You for creating in me a new heart and a right spirit that is willing and obedient to you. In Jesus' name. Amen.

You are now a new creation in Christ! Remember this day.

Sign_______________________________________

Date_______________________________________

Check this out to find a local church body in your area:

https://www.rhema.org/index.php?option=com_wrapper&view=wrapper&Itemid=114

Please do not forsake the assembling of yourself together as is the manner of some (Hebrews 10:25). You have received Jesus as Lord, make sure you check with Him on where to go. He will tell you. Trust and listen to Him.

Anna White is President of Anna White Ministries and the founder of 4GIVEN located in Bixby, OK. For questions or if you would like to book Anna White

Write to:

Anna White Ministries

16 S A Ave #605

Bixby, OK. 74008

4giveninc@gmail.com

(918) 703-3249

https://www.4giveninc.com

Books By Anna E. White

What's The Big Deal?

Why Do I Have To Obey My Parents?

Why Can't I Do Whatever I Want?

Cooking with Ms. Anna

Josiah Brushes His Teeth

www.ingramcontent.com/pod-product-compliance
Lightning Source LLC
Chambersburg PA
CBHW070755160726
48004CB00001B/203